Massachusetts

BY AMY VAN ZEE

Published by The Child's World®
1980 Lookout Drive • Mankato, MN 56003-1705
800-599-READ • www.childsworld.com

ACKNOWLEDGMENTS
The Child's World®: Mary Berendes, Publishing Director
The Design Lab: Design and production
Red Line Editorial: Editorial direction

PHOTO CREDITS: Jorge Salcedo/Dreamstime, cover, 1, 3; Matt Kania/
Map Hero, Inc., 4, 5; Jorge Salcedo/Shutterstock Images, 7; Jim Lozouski/
Shutterstock Images, 9; iStockphoto, 10; Mona Plougmann/iStockphoto, 11;
Charles Krupa/AP Images, 13; North Wind Picture Archives/AP Images, 15;
Michael Dwyer/AP Images, 17; AP Images, 19; Chee-Onn Leong/Shutterstock
Images, 21; One Mile Up, 22; Quarter-dollar coin image from the United
States Mint, 22

LIBRARY OF CONGRESS CATALOGING-IN-PUBLICATION DATA
Van Zee, Amy.
  Massachusetts / by Amy Van Zee.
      p. cm.
  Includes bibliographical references and index.
  ISBN 978-1-60253-465-0 (library bound : alk. paper)
  1. Massachusetts—Juvenile literature. I. Title.

  F64.3.V36 2010
  974.4—dc22

                      2010017717

Printed in the United States of America in Mankato, Minnesota.
July 2010
F11538

On the cover: The
Old North Church
and a statue
of Paul Revere
are in Boston,
Massachusetts.

CONTENTS

4 Geography

6 Cities

8 Land

10 Plants and Animals

12 People and Work

14 History

16 Ways of Life

18 Famous People

20 Famous Places

22 *State Symbols*

23 *Glossary*

24 *Further Information*

24 *Index*

Geography

Let's explore Massachusetts! Massachusetts is in the northeastern United States. This area is called New England. The Atlantic Ocean is to the east of the state.

VERMONT

NEW HAMPSHIRE

NEW YORK

Atlantic
Ocean

Greenfield

Lowell

Gloucester

Leominster

Salem

Cambridge

MASSACHUSETTS

*Freedom
Trail*

Massachusetts
Bay

Boston

Worcester

Springfield

Plymouth

Carver

RHODE
ISLAND

Onset

New
Bedford

Barnstable
Town

CONNECTICUT

*Martha's
Vineyard*

Nantucket

NEW YORK

NORTH

WEST   EAST

SOUTH

5

Cities

Boston is the capital of Massachusetts. It is also the state's largest city. Cambridge, Worcester, and Springfield are other large cities in the state.

Boston is located on Massachusetts Bay, ▶ which connects to the Atlantic Ocean.

Land

Massachusetts has mountains, hills, valleys, and islands. Its two main islands are Nantucket and Martha's Vineyard. The state has about 190 miles (306 km) of coastline. This area is flat. The state also has many lakes and streams.

The Assabet River runs through Massachusetts. ▶

Plants and Animals

The black-capped chickadee is the Massachusetts state bird. Its song can sound like a whistle. The mayflower is the state flower. It is white or pink. The American elm is the state tree. Its wood is good for making furniture.

The mayflower opens in the spring. ▶

People and Work

Almost 6.5 million people live in Massachusetts. Many people work in jobs that help **tourists** who visit the state. Many products are also made here. These include paper, tools, and jewelry.

Many cranberries are grown in Massachusetts. ▶
This man harvests the fruit in Carver.

History

In the 1620s, people from England sailed to North America. Many of them landed in the Massachusetts area. These people formed the Massachusetts Bay **Colony**. Later, people living in the area no longer liked England's laws and taxes. They met to talk about becoming free from England. The colonists became free after winning the **American Revolution**. Many battles were fought in Massachusetts. It became the sixth state on February 6, 1788.

Colonists in Massachusetts threw British tea into Boston Harbor in 1773. ▶

A group of people in Massachusetts boarded British ships that carried tea. They then threw the tea into the water. This was called the Boston Tea Party. These people were upset by the British taxes on tea and other things they used.

Ways of Life

Many people visit Massachusetts to see its historical places. Some visit **museums**, **libraries**, forests, lakes, and beaches. The Tanglewood Music **Festival** is one **popular** event. It is held during the summer.

Many people in Massachusetts take part in acting out battles of the American Revolution. ▶

Famous People

John Adams, John Quincy Adams, John F. Kennedy, and George H. W. Bush were born in Massachusetts. Each was a U.S. president. Emily Dickinson was also born in Massachusetts. She wrote many **poems** that have become well known. Benjamin Franklin was born in this state, too.

John F. Kennedy was the thirty-fifth president of the United States. He was president from 1961 to 1963. ▶

Famous Places

Many famous colleges and universities are in Massachusetts. Visitors can also see the **Minute Man** National Historical Park. This includes the site of one of the first battles of the American Revolution. On the Freedom Trail in Boston, visitors can see other sights that were important during this time period.

The Old State House in Boston was once the British government's main building in the colonies. Visitors can see ▶ this and 15 other historical sites on the Freedom Trail.

State Symbols

Seal

The state seal contains a Latin **motto** that means, "By the sword we seek peace, but peace only under liberty." Go to childsworld.com/links for a link to Massachusetts's state Web site, where you can get a firsthand look at the state seal.

Flag

The seal is on the state flag. The flag was approved in 1971.

Quarter

The Massachusetts state quarter shows a Minute Man. It came out in 2000.

Glossary

American Revolution (uh-MER-ih-kin rev-uh-LOO-shun): During the American Revolution, from 1775 to 1783, the 13 American colonies fought against Britain for their independence. Many events of the American Revolution took place in Massachusetts.

colony (KOL-uh-nee): A colony is an area of land that is newly settled and is controlled by a government of another land. The Massachusetts Bay Colony was a large American colony.

festival (FESS-tih-vul): A festival is a celebration for an event or holiday. The Tanglewood Music Festival is held in Massachusetts each year.

libraries (LY-brayr-eez): Libraries are places where books, magazines, and other items can be borrowed. Massachusetts has many libraries to visit.

Minute Man (MIN-it MAN): A Minute Man was a volunteer soldier during the American Revolution. The Minute Man National Historical Park is in Massachusetts.

motto (MOT-oh): A motto is a sentence that states what people stand for or believe. The motto for Massachusetts is "By the sword we seek peace, but peace only under liberty."

museums (myoo-ZEE-umz): Museums are places where people go to see art, history, or science displays. Many people visit the museums in Massachusetts.

poems (POH-umz): Poems are pieces of writing that often have short lines and sometimes rhyme. Emily Dickinson, who was from Massachusetts, wrote poems.

popular (POP-yuh-lur): To be popular is to be enjoyed by many people. Massachusetts holds a popular music event each year.

seal (SEEL): A seal is a symbol a state uses for government business. The Massachusetts seal has a Latin motto on it.

symbols (SIM-bulz): Symbols are pictures or things that stand for something else. The seal and the flag are symbols of Massachusetts.

tourists (TOOR-ists): Tourists are people who visit a place (such as a state or country) for fun. Many tourists visit Massachusetts to see its historic sites.

Further Information

Books

De Capua, Sarah. *Massachusetts*. New York: Children's Press, 2002.

Raven, Margaret Theis. *M is for Mayflower: A Massachusetts Alphabet*. Chelsea, MI: Sleeping Bear Press, 2002.

Reynolds, Jeff. *A to Z: United States of America*. New York: Children's Press, 2002.

Web Sites

Visit our Web site for links about Massachusetts: *childsworld.com/links*

Note to Parents, Teachers, and Librarians: We routinely verify our Web links to make sure they are safe and active sites. So encourage your readers to check them out!

Index

American Revolution, 14, 20
Atlantic Ocean, 4
capital, 6
Freedom Trail, 20
jobs, 12
Martha's Vineyard, 8

Massachusetts Bay Colony, 14
Minute Man National Historic Park, 20
Nantucket, 8
New England, 4
population, 12

state bird, 10
state flower, 10
state tree, 10
Tanglewood Music Festival, 16
tourism, 12, 16, 20
U.S. presidents, 18